EXPLORING THE STATES

Delaware

THE FIRST STATE

by Emily Schnobrich

BLASTOFF!
5
READERS

BELLWETHER MEDIA • MINNEAPOLIS, MN

Note to Librarians, Teachers, and Parents:

Blastoff! Readers are carefully developed by literacy experts and combine standards-based content with developmentally appropriate text.

Level 1 provides the most support through repetition of high-frequency words, light text, predictable sentence patterns, and strong visual support.

Level 2 offers early readers a bit more challenge through varied simple sentences, increased text load, and less repetition of high-frequency words.

Level 3 advances early-fluent readers toward fluency through increased text and concept load, less reliance on visuals, longer sentences, and more literary language.

Level 4 builds reading stamina by providing more text per page, increased use of punctuation, greater variation in sentence patterns, and increasingly challenging vocabulary.

Level 5 encourages children to move from "learning to read" to "reading to learn" by providing even more text, varied writing styles, and less familiar topics.

Whichever book is right for your reader, Blastoff! Readers are the perfect books to build confidence and encourage a love of reading that will last a lifetime!

This edition first published in 2014 by Bellwether Media, Inc.

No part of this publication may be reproduced in whole or in part without written permission of the publisher. For information regarding permission, write to Bellwether Media, Inc., Attention: Permissions Department, 5357 Penn Avenue South, Minneapolis, MN 55419.

Library of Congress Cataloging-in-Publication Data

Schnobrich, Emily.
  Delaware / by Emily Schnobrich.
     pages cm. – (Blastoff! readers. Exploring the states)
  Includes bibliographical references and index.
  Summary: "Developed by literacy experts for students in grades three through seven, this book introduces young readers to the geography and culture of Delaware"–Provided by publisher.
  ISBN 978-1-62617-007-0 (hardcover : alk. paper)
  1. Delaware–Juvenile literature. I. Title.
  F164.3.S37 2014
  975.1–dc23
                                                                    2013008948

Printed in the United States of America, North Mankato, MN.

Table of Contents

Where Is Delaware?

Delaware is a small state in the middle of the Atlantic Coast of the United States. Most of it lies within the Delmarva **Peninsula**. Delaware shares this piece of land with Maryland and Virginia. Maryland hugs Delaware to the west and south. Pennsylvania is its neighbor to the north. The Delaware Bay separates the state from New Jersey in the east.

Delaware is the second smallest state in the country. However, it lies close to some of the nation's largest cities. Dover, the state capital, is just three hours away from New York City.

Virginia

Pennsylvania

Delaware River

N
W · E
S

● Wilmington

● Newark

↑ Chesapeake
and Delaware
Canal

New Jersey

★ Dover

Delaware Bay

Atlantic Ocean

Delaware

Maryland

← Chesapeake
Bay

Native Americans such as the Lenni-Lenape and Nanticoke lived in Delaware long ago. In the 1600s, Dutch and Swedish people settled the land. Later the British took control. During the **Revolutionary War**, Delaware joined the other **colonies** to fight for independence. It became the first state to approve the United States **Constitution** in 1787.

**Henry Hudson
explores Delaware**

Delaware Timeline!

1609: Henry Hudson is the first European to explore Delaware.

1638: Swedes begin the first permanent European settlement in Delaware.

1664: England takes control of Delaware.

1776: Delawarean Caesar Rodney rides to Philadelphia to vote for independence from Britain.

1787: Delaware becomes the first U.S. state.

1829: The Chesapeake and Delaware Canal opens.

1935: A worker at the DuPont company invents nylon, a flexible material with many uses.

1951: The Delaware Memorial Bridge opens near Wilmington. It allows cars to travel across the Delaware River to New Jersey.

2000: Ruth Ann Minner becomes Delaware's first female governor.

Caesar Rodney

nylon invention

Ruth Ann Minner

The Land

Delaware's entire eastern border touches water. **Marshes** dominate the Delaware Bay shoreline. The Delaware River and other smaller **tributaries** empty into this body of water. In the southeast, more than 20 miles (32 kilometers) of sandy beaches run along the Atlantic Coast.

Delaware is very flat. Farmland and woods cover the south. Rolling hills stretch down from the north. The Chesapeake and Delaware **Canal** slices across Delaware's northern tip. Nearby, the land rises to its highest point of only 448 feet (137 meters). Delaware is warm and breezy in summer. Winters are mild and snowy.

Delaware River

Delaware's Climate

average °F

spring
Low: 42°
High: 62°

summer
Low: 65°
High: 84°

fall
Low: 47°
High: 66°

winter
Low: 26°
High: 42°

Did you know?
Delaware has the second lowest land of any U.S. state. Only Florida is lower.

Chesapeake and Delaware Canal

The Chesapeake and Delaware Canal is an important human-made waterway. It stretches from the Chesapeake Bay in Maryland to the Delaware River in Delaware. This shortens the shipping route between the two bodies of water by about 300 miles (483 kilometers).

The canal is 14 miles (23 kilometers) long and 450 feet (137 meters) wide. Five different bridges span it. The C&D Canal Trail runs alongside the waterway. People can cycle, stroll, or picnic along the path.

Wildlife

One-third of Delaware is covered in forests. Bald cypress trees stretch their limbs in southern swamps. Tangled thickets of blueberries and cranberries grow nearby. Deer, gray foxes, and mink search for food in the woods and fields. Hawks and cardinals fly overhead.

Fishers catch bass, catfish, and trout in the state's rivers and lakes. Muskrats and snapping turtles splash around in coastal marshes. Along the shore, **migrating** sandpipers fill up on crab eggs. Several types of sharks give birth to pups in Delaware Bay. Lucky sightseers may even spot humpback whales in late summer.

mink

snapping turtle

horseshoe crab

fun fact

The world's largest population of horseshoe crabs lives in Delaware Bay. They gather on the beach to mate every spring.

sandpiper

Dover International Speedway

Delaware is known for the Dover International Speedway. This oval track hosts thrilling car races every year. At Trap Pond State Park, visitors can bird-watch and see bald cypress trees growing from the water. Cape Henlopen State Park offers twisting hiking trails, shimmering beaches, and stunning views of Delaware Bay.

Winterthur
Museum

Miles the Monster

fun fact

Miles the Monster guards the Dover
International Speedway. He earned his
name from the racetrack's nickname,
the Monster Mile. It is the fastest
one-mile oval racetrack in the world!

Some of Delaware's historic buildings now operate as
museums. The Winterthur Museum in Wilmington features
furniture, silverware, and other **decorative arts**.
Visitors can experience the state's farming heritage at the
Delaware Agricultural Museum and Village in Dover.

Wilmington

Wilmington is the largest city in Delaware. It is located in the north along the Delaware River. Long ago, a group of brave Swedish settlers built the first log cabins in Wilmington. Today, visitors can tour the original spot at Fort Christina State Park. Wilmington is also an important **port city**. Ships come and go with automobiles and other products.

Wilmington is home to the Delaware Museum of Natural History. Dinosaur skeletons and life-size models of **exotic** creatures fill the rooms. Children love the magical Enchanted Woods at Winterthur Museum and Garden. They climb into the Tulip Tree House and explore the garden maze.

Fort Christina

New Castle

fun fact

South of Wilmington sits the historic town of New Castle. Its streets are lined with homes and buildings that are hundreds of years old.

Delaware is home to several large chemical companies. They hire workers to make a variety of products, such as **nylon**, rubber, and medicine. The state's bankers run credit card companies and help people manage their money.

Farmers in Delaware raise chickens to sell all over the country. They also grow rows of soybeans, corn, and other vegetables. Many Delawareans serve **tourists** at hotels and restaurants. Others work hard to protect plants and animals in parks and wildlife areas. Off the coast, fishers pull in heavy catches of clams and blue crabs.

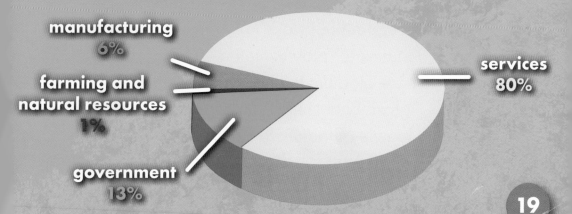

Where People Work in Delaware

manufacturing
6%

farming and
natural resources
1%

government
13%

services
80%

Playing

Rehoboth Beach

Delawareans love to stroll the beaches in summer. At Rehoboth Beach, people splash in the ocean while others surf, watch dolphins, or play miniature golf nearby. Sports fans fill Delaware Stadium to cheer for the University of Delaware's Fightin' Blue Hens football team. Baseball lovers crowd Frawley Stadium to see the Blue Rocks minor league team play.

Blue Hens football

geocaching

Delaware's state parks and woodlands are perfect for bird-watching, hiking, and camping. Some Delawareans float the waterways in kayaks or take boats out to sea. Adventurers enjoy an outdoor treasure hunt called **geocaching**. They use **GPS** devices to search for items scattered throughout the state.

Crab Puffs

Ingredients:

Cooking oil

2 cups flour

3 teaspoons baking powder

1/2 teaspoon salt

1 egg

1 cup milk

1/2 pound crabmeat

Directions:

1. Heat cooking oil to 375°F.

2. Mix the flour, baking powder, and salt.

3. In a separate bowl, beat the egg. Add the milk and crabmeat. Stir into the flour mixture. Mix well.

4. Drop the mixture from a spoon into hot oil. Fry until delicately browned.

seafood stew

! fun fact

The Wagon Wheel Restaurant in Smyrna has muskrat on the menu! It is usually served with stewed tomatoes.

Delawareans can't get enough seafood. Fishers haul in crabs, shrimp, clams, and fish to eat. Cooks make fluffy crab puffs and hot seafood stew. Delawareans also cook up **broiler chickens**, often with biscuits or vegetables. Slippery dumplings are popular in the south. These flat squares of dough are cooked in chicken broth to make them rich and slippery.

Juicy peaches and apples hang from trees, and berries grow near the ground. Many people like to cook these fruits into desserts or jams. Delawareans also love lima beans, sweet corn, and fresh tomatoes. They often preserve these vegetables to enjoy in the middle of winter.

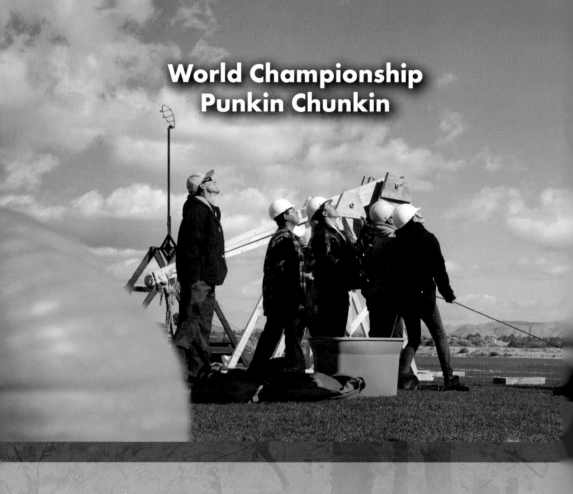

World Championship Punkin Chunkin

Every May, Delawareans celebrate the nation's first state at the Dover Days Festival. For music lovers, Dover's three-day Firefly Festival is a great part of summer. Visitors camp and relax on picnic blankets while popular musicians perform outside. Delawareans also watch exciting **NASCAR** races twice a year at the Dover International Speedway.

Firefly Festival

Each fall, Rehoboth Beach becomes a magical place for the Sea Witch Halloween and Fiddler's Festival. Children and adults compete in cackle contests, watch magic shows, and dress up their dogs for a costume parade. One of Delaware's funniest **traditions** is the World Championship Punkin Chunkin. Teams compete to see who can fire a pumpkin the farthest using a machine!

Nemours Mansion and Gardens

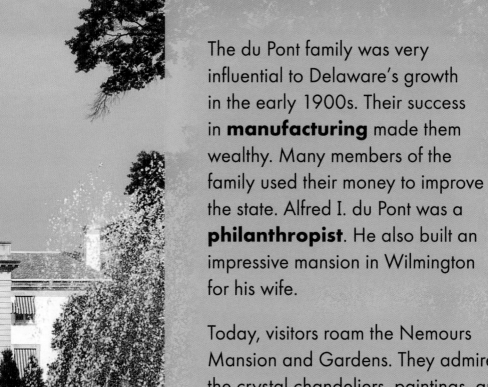

The du Pont family was very influential to Delaware's growth in the early 1900s. Their success in **manufacturing** made them wealthy. Many members of the family used their money to improve the state. Alfred I. du Pont was a **philanthropist**. He also built an impressive mansion in Wilmington for his wife.

Today, visitors roam the Nemours Mansion and Gardens. They admire the crystal chandeliers, paintings, and historical furniture inside the mansion. Outside, the gardens are filled with statues, trees, and fountains. The Nemours Mansion is an elegant piece of Delaware's history.

! fun fact

A long reflecting pool in the gardens holds 800,000 gallons (3,028,329 liters) of water. It takes three days to fill!

Fast Facts About Delaware

DECEMBER 7, 1787

Delaware's Flag

Delaware's flag is blue. The state seal sits inside a large tan diamond in the center of the flag. The seal features a soldier and a farmer. Between the two figures are a ship, a bundle of wheat, an ear of corn, and an ox. These items symbolize Delaware's economy and resources. A banner below them holds the state motto. Near the bottom of the flag is the date Delaware adopted the U.S. Constitution.

State Flower
peach blossom

State Nicknames:	The First State The Diamond State
State Motto:	"Liberty and Independence"
Year of Statehood:	1787
Capital City:	Dover
Other Major Cities:	Wilmington, Newark
Population:	897,934 (2010)
Area:	2,023 square miles (5,240 square kilometers); Delaware is the 2nd smallest state.
Major Industries:	chemical manufacturing, banking, services, farming
Natural Resources:	sand, gravel, magnesium
State Government:	41 representatives; 21 senators
Federal Government:	1 representative; 2 senators
Electoral Votes:	3

State Animal
gray fox

State Bird
Blue Hen chicken

Glossary

broiler chickens—chickens raised specifically for meat

canal—a waterway that is built to connect larger bodies of water

colonies—territories owned and settled by people from another country

constitution—the basic principles and laws of a nation

decorative arts—art that is useful, such as furniture

exotic—originally from another country

geocaching—an outdoor activity that involves searching for hidden objects

GPS—a system that shows users exactly where they are on Earth; GPS stands for Global Positioning System.

manufacturing—a field of work in which people use machines to make products

marshes—wetlands with grasses and plants

migrating—traveling from one place to another, often with the seasons

NASCAR—National Association for Stock Car Auto Racing

native—originally from a specific place

nylon—a strong, stretchy material that can be made into other things

peninsula—a section of land that extends out from a larger piece of land and is almost completely surrounded by water

philanthropist—a person who donates money or resources to a good cause

port city—a city with a harbor where ships can dock

Revolutionary War—the war between 1775 and 1783 in which the United States fought for independence from Great Britain

tourists—people who travel to visit another place

traditions—customs, ideas, or beliefs handed down from one generation to the next

tributaries—streams or rivers that flow into larger bodies of water

To Learn More

AT THE LIBRARY

Price Hossell, Karen. *Delaware, 1638-1776*. Washington, D.C.: National Geographic Society, 2006.

Williams, Carol L. *The Rescue Begins in Delaware*. Sanger, Calif.: Familius, 2013.

Winans, Jay D. *Delaware: The First State*. New York, N.Y.: AV2 by Weigl, 2012.

ON THE WEB

Learning more about Delaware is as easy as 1, 2, 3.

1. Go to www.factsurfer.com.

2. Enter "Delaware" into the search box.

3. Click the "Surf" button and you will see a list of related Web sites.

With factsurfer.com, finding more information is just a click away.

Index

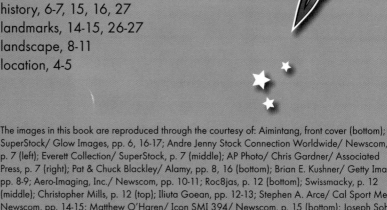

The images in this book are reproduced through the courtesy of: Aimintang, front cover (bottom); SuperStock/ Glow Images, pp. 6, 16-17; Andre Jenny Stock Connection Worldwide/ Newscom, p. 7 (left); Everett Collection/ SuperStock, p. 7 (middle); AP Photo/ Chris Gardner/ Associated Press, p. 7 (right); Pat & Chuck Blackley/ Alamy, pp. 8, 16 (bottom); Brian E. Kushner/ Getty Images, pp. 8-9; Aero-Imaging, Inc./ Newscom, pp. 10-11; Roc8jas, p. 12 (bottom); Swissmacky, p. 12 (middle); Christopher Mills, p. 12 (top); Iliuta Goean, pp. 12-13; Stephen A. Arce/ Cal Sport Media/ Newscom, pp. 14-15; Matthew O'Haren/ Icon SMI 394/ Newscom, p. 15 (bottom); Joseph Sohm Visions of America/ Newscom, p. 15 (top); Visions of America/ Glow Images, p. 16 (top); Monty Rakusen/ Glow Images, p. 18; Dmitry Kalinovsky, p. 19; AP Photo/ Daily Times, Chuck Snyder/ Associated Press, pp. 20-21; Saquan Stimpson/ Newscom, p. 22 (top); Saltcityphotography/ Dreamstime.com, p. 21 (bottom); M. Unal Ozmaen, p. 22 (top); Olga Popova, p. 22 (middle); Maks Narodenko, p. 22 (bottom); Marco Mayer, p. 23; AP Photo/ The Victor Valley Daily Press, James Quigg/ Associated Press, pp. 24-25; Getty Images, p. 25; Mira/ Alamy, pp. 26-27; Pakmor, p. 28 (top); Oleksii Sagitov, p. 28 (bottom); Age Fotostock/ SuperStock, p. 29 (left); Carlos Ameglio/ Dreamstime.com, p. 29 (right).